Stoicism Full Life Mastery: Mastering The Stoic Way Of Living And Emotions

licensed professional before attempting any techniques outlined in this book.

By reading this document, the reader agrees that under no circumstances are is the author responsible for any losses, direct or indirect, which are incurred as a result of the use of information contained within this document, including, but not limited to, —errors, omissions, or inaccuracies.

Introduction

Stoicism is getting popular these days. Perhaps it is because we are increasingly aware of the laws of nature and how much of them are completely out of our control. Maybe it's because many folks believe our society has been getting softer and softer, and we need a philosophy that can toughen up a few people. Or because we live in a world that is so complex, so full of noise, stimulus, contrasting emotions and feelings, that we feel the need to retreat within ourselves and by guided by a trusted philosophy of self-enhancement.

Stoicism has an interesting story, having been able to seduce both Emperors and slaves alike. But it was never a philosophy easy to abide by and requires many personal sacrifices and self-discipline, two words our current society seems to loathe. Yet, as is the case of most major religions and spiritual quests, these kind of processes are crucial for the betterment of our character.

This book intends to introduce you to the philosophy of stoicism, its history, major principles, techniques, exercises and advices for our modern world. Whether you are just curious about this philosophy or whether you feel ready to undertake a major life transformation that could lead to greater happiness and peace of mind, you will find this book useful. As a Stoic beginner, you will probably struggle with some concepts, but we tried to provide you with concrete examples to help you.

Chapter 1 Common Philosophies of Stoicism

Stoicism is an ancient philosophy that was born in Ancient Greece. From the Ancient Greek Culture, stoicism kept the respect for reasoning and logic but also certain mystical beliefs in a predetermined world order. As a philosophy that was highly influential in its time and continues to be so until this day, there have been many writings and interpretations of it.

The most common philosophy of stoicism relates to ethics, mostly because it was very influential to Roman Emperor Marcus. But stoicism is a complex philosophical system and it does not simply tell us how to act, but also provides a global framework in which every living creature operates.

Because ethics in philosophy is usually the end and not the starting point, we should go about it the traditional way and begin by explaining the tenets of stoic philosophy : Metaphysics.

STOIC METAPHYSICS (and physics)

In the ancient world, physics and metaphysics were hard to tell apart, mostly because the physical order usually required metaphysical laws to make sense. The stoics were no exception, and because of that we should englobe into the stoic metaphysics their physical system as well.

The universe itself is considered to be a pantheistic God which is, actually, the material-divine substance of pneuma, a kind of breath of life or divine essence. When matter separates from force, a divine fire called aether is produced. The pneuma then acts on this aether according to the logos or divine reason of the universe, causing the processes of formation, development and destruction

Pneuma, due to its active components, was the cause for action in the universe. What this meant is that pneuma was responsible for the distinctive traits of individual personalities, for example, that cause us beings of the earth to act in a number of different but peculiar ways. It is present in plants and animals, but the only being with the faculty of reasoning is the human being.

The identity of individuals, therefore, was a simple bundle of qualities and properties established by the pneuma within them as an emanation of the aether of the universe. These were not chosen or created by the individual itself, but they formed the inalterable core of his identity.

The stoics believed, therefore, that all things that exist are, in end, material things - even if their definition of material involved a divine essence impregnated in every single substance. Emotions are material things as well, the proof of that is their physical manifestation - feeling scared and sweating, for example. Our body produces sense impressions in the soul, which produces movements in the body. Therefore, for the stoics, they must be made of the same thing, have the same principle, otherwise communication between them would be impossible.

 All things are subjected to Fate, since the entire world is constantly emanating from just one principle. You can imagine the universe as some sort of breathing living body, with all different parts interconnected to the point that one must clearly influence the other. Everything is predetermined, even though humans are thought to have some degree of free will when it comes to their acceptance or denial of this harsh reality.

The stoics believed that the universe exist within a temporal never-ending cycle of formation and destruction. It came from fire - the aether - and it will return to fire and then be born again, forever.

All these beliefs might sound strange to us, because Western society core perceptions of reality have been influenced mainly by the Christian worldview. However, in many "pagan" societies and particularly in Ancient Greece, the ideal of a founding principle of the universe without a "maker" or "creator" in the Christian sense of the word, and of history as a never-ending cycle, are rather common intuitions. In fact, many of the ideas of the stoics can be traced back to other philosophers of Ancient Greece, such as Heraclitus or Aristotle. The focus on logos as a founding force of the universe, a divine intelligence or order if you will, is also a very Greek thing.

STOIC EPISTEMOLOGY

How is knowledge possible? When and how can we actually say, with conviction, that we *know* something and that statement is true? What is the connection between our minds and the outside world that allows us to inquire factually about what surrounds us?

The stoics were empiricists. This means they based most of their theory of knowledge in experience and perception, rather than idealized abstract theories. If Plato and Aristotle were soccer teams, the stoics would firmly stand by Aristotle is what their theory of knowledge is concerned.

But since they came after Socrates and the skeptics, two philosophical forces that shook the core beliefs and forever raised doubts about the validity of our convictions, the stoics were very much concerned about the possibility of error and how to fix it.

Let us start with the basics. As we have previously mentioned, the stoics believe everything to be matter, including thoughts and emotions. We are constantly bombarded with impressions, called phantasia by the stoics - we have the impression of a tree, of a color, of the weather, of sadness, of another person's presence. But not all of those impressions are true. We can mistake the kind of tree it is or realize the another person's presence was nothing but a shadow, for example.

The stoics, the standard of truth regarding impressions was whether or not they were comprehensible - something akin to Locke's clear and distinct ideas. You know, more or less instinctively, whether what you are seeing is the truth. These are defined as impressions of what it is for what it is, distinctive and sealed. The object of your impression is 100% compatible to the object in the outside world and you are sure of this.

Non-cataleptic impressions, therefore, are those which are confused and raise doubts, that cause us to take something for what it isn't.

The skeptics of antiquity had a field day with this theory. For skeptics, all impressions are acataleptic. You just can never be sure of whether or not you are absorbing reality for what it is, you are caught in a world of feeble representations and half-truths. The stoics, due to their metaphysical system and beliefs, did believed in truth and that you could grasp it.

But, perhaps influenced by the skeptics, the stoics firmly held that no one could be right all the time. Even the great sages made mistakes. They assumed people often made mistakes regarding the clearness and distinctiveness of impressions, which were quickly shown to be problematic after scrutiny and investigation. In this case, what do the stoics defined as knowledge? Something grasped in a such a way that could not be shaken by argument, according to Cicero.

This criteria is quite difficult to abide to. It means the vast majority of people are not wise or knowledgeable, since, as Socrates clearly showed, most of their beliefs cannot be subjected to logical inquiry or arguments without disintegrating completely.

On the topic of argumentation, the stoics were star philosophers of logic as well, devising a unique system to analyze the veracity of arguments based on their composition.

STOIC LOGIC

Stoic logic is a propositional logic, meaning it is concerned with the value (true or false) of affirmations or propositions. Whatever you say when you are describing, affirming, making an inquiry or an oath, etc., has either one of those properties of true or false in the given moment. These properties might change - for now, this tree is small, in a couple of years this tree is big.

The stoics mostly used a combination of propositions to prove arguments, but they incorporated their own metaphysical beliefs into logic. The most important one was the belief in causal determinism, meaning everything need to have an antecedent cause in order for it to exist. Most stoic logic, therefore, is more interested in the validity of arguments and not necessarily on logical theorems or truths. As always, their goal was for logic to be practical.

Their logic is very complex, incorporating grammar and rhetoric. Unless you have prior knowledge of logic as a philosophical subject, it might not be as relevant.

STOIC POLITICAL THEORY

All great philosophical systems of Ancient Greece were deeply political. There are some exceptions - like the Cynics - who despised the city or *polis*, but the stoics, perhaps because so many of their main thinkers were directly involved in governing during the Roman Empire, viewed politics as an essential part of human life.

The same way the universe was viewed as a unity, with an internal logic and determination of events, the civil society was also a unite brotherhood of men. The stoics were egalitarians and viewed the state as a natural occurrence. Everyone must abide by the same principles of living and attempt to have a unified human society. There is one major exception, of course: the king, He who yields all the power and who is the state embodied.

The king is a symbolic figure of harmony and divinity and He establishes the natural order of things. If you disobey the king, you are not only a criminal, but you are anti-nature, which in stoic metaphysics is akin to being anti-God. As the representative of the divine order on Earth, the king is the keeper of morality, religion and ethics.

As long as there is a king and this harmony is maintained, the stoics did not take issue with people from different city-states or nations. Since the same divine reason is said to rule all men, in particular those who are representatives of the order of the world, you cannot just go around changing it. The law directs what must be done and forbids that which cannot be done.

In this way, not only did stoic political theory create a mostly egalitarian society with a head of state at the top, it also wanted to bring about the harmony of the states between themselves. Each man is governed by the law of nature/reason and the law of custom/the law of the city. Obviously, the law of custom or city is fashioned in accordance to the law of nature and each state is thought to conform to that. You could say customs are but a local interpretation of a cosmopolitan order.

If you think about it, the stoics would not look down on our globalized world. In fact, it was very much their vision. There are international laws created by reason and then local laws. There are human rights that are meant to equalize every single person and then there are other sorts of rights, obligations and prohibitions - at least in theory respectful of basic human rights - that are applied in specific areas of the world.

Stoic philosophers did not make all the people be the same, they were clearly aware of differences of character and virtue and of those of a lesser kind, like property or finances. But the principles of nature make no distinction and that is the rule by which we should live - by focusing too much on differences, the harmony of society can be threatened.

It is interesting to see how the stoics were able to create such a cosmopolitan political theory that pays absolutely no attention to the individual. Some stoics even went as far as suggesting certain things should be shared, like wives or property.

Still, holding that the world order can only be maintained through an absolute king was quite reactionary, even in Ancient Greece. It is a symptom of the crisis felt, when the Western world was undergoing a slow transition to an international empire and looking for concrete standards with which to value their lives.

Of course, the stoics also had a proposal for that - their system of ethics.

MAIN THINKERS

Ethics is probably the most important and influential branch of the stoic system. The remaining of this book will focus mainly on ethics, since stoic physical doctrine has been mostly debunked by modern science, logic has evolved dramatically and although ideas of law and equality are still present in Western society, we are mostly done with dictators and absolute monarchies. Before presenting you their ethical system, however, it is better to introduce the main thinkers of stoicism since each of them added to stoic ethics and enriched its development. Then, we will give you some basic information about the lasting influence of stoicism before tackling ethics head-on.

The main thinkers of the stoic philosophical system were, by chronological order:

ZENO OF CITIUM (334 - 262 BC)

Zeno was the founder of stoicism. The name is derived from the place where he used the teach his disciples, the StoaPoikile in the Agora of Ancient Athens. The Stoa was simply a porch.

Zeno was born in Citium, modern Cyprus, making him a Phoenician and not an Athenian. Although he became a rich merchant, people from the time usually describe him as ascetic and a haggard. He studied under several philosophical schools until he decided to take up teaching himself. His reputation grew far and wide, collecting sophisticated fans like the king of Macedonia. He was showered with honors by the Athenians and was even proposed to become a citizen, but refuse out of loyalty for his native land. He was a man of few and important words and disliked those who speak too much for nothing.

CATO THE YOUNGER (95 BC - 46 BC)

Cato, born almost two centuries after Zeno, was already a Roman citizen. The son of a celebrated politician whose live was cut short, he lived his early years in Rome in close contact with the Imperial family. He started studying stoicism as a young man and was deeply devoted to the stoic doctrine and to the Roman Republic, having lived through times of turmoil and civil war after its deterioration. He was the first stoic to become an actual politician, a full-grown Roman senator, applying the stoic principles to governance and the defense of what he considered to be essential Roman principles of statehood.

Cato was one of Julius Caesar's main opponents. As a stern defender of the Republic, his myth lived on to inspire one of Cato's biggest admirers, George Washington.

SENECA (4 BC - 65 AD)

Seneca is an interesting character in Roman history. Because he was the political advisor of the infamous Nero, the Roman Emperor that burned the Imperial city to the grown - so the legend goes - and tactically agreeing to the murder of Nero's mother Agrippina. Seneca was also accused of being corrupt due to his immense wealth and close relations with at least two emperors. Seneca felt so wounded by these accusations he actually wrote a stoic defense of wealth in order to justify himself. In short, Seneca seemed to embody the best and worst of a politician. However, he was a great writer and eloquent philosopher.

Born in modern Spain, Seneca was mostly raised in an influential family in Rome. He won a seat in the Senate at a young age and despite a successful oratory skills, he was accused of adultery with a sister of Caligula and sentenced to death by the Senate. The Emperor at the time, Claudius, allowed him to live in exile. Seneca was stranded in Corsica for eight years, until Agrippina married her uncle Claudius, became empress and called Seneca back from exile. She turned Seneca into a praetor and he became her son Nero's tutor and, when Claudius died, Nero's political advisor.

In his defense, Seneca did try to retire on multiple occasions but Nero wouldn't allow him to do so. When a conspiracy to kill the mad emperor was known, Nero thought Seneca was involved and ordered him to kill himself.

EPICTETUS (55 - 135 AD)

Born a slave, Epictetus worked for most of his youth but developed a passion for philosophy early in life. His owner allowed him to study it freely, studying under an influential Roman stoic philosopher. Epictetus was freed sometime after Nero's death, already considered to be quite respectable due to his studies. He began to teach philosophy in Rome but was exiled when the Emperor Domitian banished all philosophers from the city. Epictetus retreated to Greece, where he founded a philosophical school and lived a quiet and simple life

Epictetus did not write anything - the writings attributed to him were actually notes from his most famous student, Arrian. The Emperor Hadrian was friendly towards Epictetus, as were most people who became mesmerized by his words.

MARCUS AURELIUS (121-180 AD)

Marcus Aurelius was a Roman Emperor and a devoted stoic philosopher. He became an Emperor almost by chance - he was adopted by a childless successor of the also childless Emperor

Hadrian. For two decades, Marcus Aurelius was the most powerful man in the world and he had his fair share of war and conflict to manage. Surprisingly, he proved himself worthy of the task and did not succumb to the degraded temptations that ruled over many Emperors that preceded him. If there was ever a positive embodiment of stoic political theory, that was Marcus Aurelius reign as Emperor. To this day, his *Meditations* are a paramount effort in self-perfection and self-examination, the efforts made by the "king of the world" to become more just and worthy of the title.

EVOLUTION AND INFLUENCE OF STOICISM

Stoicism also did not remain the same throughout the centuries and it had great influence on our Western culture, even though it isn't always obvious.

From the time of Zeno, stoicism was subject to change. A philosophy that began in the ancient agora and reached the peaks of power during the Roman Empire was clearly one that seeks self-perfection.

We can roughly divide the evolution of stoicism between ancient Greek stoicism, Middle Stoa or late Roman Empire stoicism and the Christian-inspired stoicism of the early Middle Ages.

Ancient Greek stoicism was scarred by the loss of the Athenian city-state as the model city, following the deaths of both Aristotle and Alexander the Great. Although it drew from ancient Greek thought and concerns, such as the importance of monism (the world emanates from one primordial substance) and the focus on human nature since Socrates. However, the two philosophical schools that influenced the stoics the most in their early stages was the Megarian school of logic and dialectics and the Cynic school and their alienating view on life.

Zeno, a former Platonist, established that philosophy should be divided in branches - ethics, physics and logic, and provided stoic principles for each of them. The successors of Zeno were mostly focused on expanding the understanding of the cosmic order and solving the logical puzzles provocatively presented by the skeptics.

During the Middle Stoa period, the stoic school was firstly devoted mostly to a quasi-religious fervor. One famous stoic from this period befriended Cicero, the Roman philosopher and writer, and the Middle Stoa is mostly characterized by the popularization of stoicism in the highest offices on the Roman Empire. As such, concerns about law, world citizenship and the divine order of reason were common during this period. Seneca, Epictetus and Marcus Aurelius largely focused on these themes.

As Christianity began to take hold of the Roman Empire during its disintegration, the Church Fathers and Christian philosophers of the early Middle Ages were influenced by stoicism and applied it - willingly or unwillingly - to many arguments regarding God's apathy, divine rule and the cosmopolitan brotherhood of men as understood by Christianity.

Nowadays, there are some attempts to rescue stoicism from the obscurity of antiquity and present it as an updated and well-informed philosophical theory. Modern stoicism was revived through the introduction of virtue ethics by a number of Anglophone philosophers, such as Martha Nussbaum and Philippa Foot. It also incorporates psychology and psychotherapy, because the stoic ethical doctrine is so dependent on our understanding of human emotions.

Modern stoicism is a movement aspiring to be universal, very dependent on the internet and various forms of social media in order for people who are interested in applying the principles of stoicism to their lives, to talk and discuss these issues freely. Obviously, given the scientific and technological advances, some portions of traditional stoicism are called into question - most of all, the original principle of the unity of a world emanating from one substance. The concept of agency is also dissected, since having some degree of free-will is a principle on which most stoic ethics stand. Lawrence C. Becker is one of the most important modern stoic philosophers working today.

Chapter 2 Virtues To Cultivate Stoicism

Talking about virtues is really talking about stoic ethics, since they make up the cornerstone of the stoic ethical system. But what exactly are virtues, to begin with? And what do they stoics mean when they say we must "cultivate" them?

These terms are ancient in itself and their roots takes us back, once again to Ancient Greece.

By virtue, we usually mean moral excellence. These are traits or characteristics in individuals we deem exceptional, and we encourage individuals to pursue them because they often equate with a great good for society. In Greek Antiquity, the virtues were a hotly debated issue, taken up by most philosophers since Socrates. Since then, they have been re-formulated a number of different times to fit the needs of different people and civilizations, but we can see some common themes.

So, in Ancient Greeks, what were often considered to be virtues? For Plato, the first philosopher to have systematized a collection of virtues to be pursued and encouraged, the classic cardinal virtues were the following: temperance, prudence, courage and justice. You will notice generosity, for example, is not in the list. The Greeks equated being virtuous as being a good leader, soldier or citizen, so the virtues were supposed to help us make informed choices about our actions, even if it meant being cruel on certain situations.

As for Aristotle, our main source of information regarding virtues in his book, the *Nicomachean Ethics*. In that classical work of philosophy and ethics, Aristotle argues that any trait can exist in excess or in deficiency, and so what we should strive for is achieving a golden mean, a perfect middle ground between excesses. That is where virtue lies.

Aristotle and Ancient Greek philosophy as a whole is suspicious of extremes. If you go into battle not caring about your life, are you really being brave or just a fool putting everyone at risk? If you do not go at all, are you just fearful or a downright coward? Being brave for Aristotle was finding the golden mean between these two examples, not being coward but also not a fool. The same applies to anything else in life, from wealth, to health, to relationships...it's about finding a balance and sticking to it, refraining from feeding your most basic instincts.

The Romans, on the other hand, were influenced by Aristotle and Plato, but developed a much bigger list of virtues. These included frugality, mercy, tenacity, justice, dutifulness, prudence, manliness, among a series of others. Some of these virtues were supposed to be applied to the private sphere only, while others were the ones required of a decent Roman citizen engaged in its society.

Virtues have also made an appearance in religious thought, usually in juxtaposition with their ugly sisters, the vices. For Judaism, for example, the most informed sources of virtues can be found in the Ten Commandments, although the virtue of wisdom seems to take a central role from which all others are derived from.

In Christianity, we found the familiar list of the seven virtues and seven vices, very present in our culture, but there are three additional ones related to how humans should act towards the divine. The three theological virtues are as follows: hope, love and faith. The seven virtues and seven vices are the following: humility/pride; kindness/envy; temperance/gluttony; chastity/lust; patience/wrath, charity/greed; diligence/sloth.

As we can see, some of them might remind us of the virtues from Antiquity, while others - mostly the ones related to the sexual sphere, are very much Christian and were added during the systematization of virtues during the Middle Ages.

Other religious or spiritual systems, such as Islam, Buddhism, Daoism or Hinduism also have their own virtues. A common trope among all religious, however, is the respect for the so called Golden Rule - that you should not do to others what others do to you, in its negative form, or you should do to others what you wish others would do to you, in its positive form.

Now, you might be wondering why I am rambling about so many different virtues. I am doing that because Stoicism has a unique categorization of virtues and in order for us to see how special that is, we have to be aware of the various systems in place stoicism has competed against throughout the centuries.

So, what are the stoic virtues? I will give you a brief list, then I will explain you what it means to "cultivate" a virtue and then I will show you how exactly can we cultivate the stoic virtues.

Stoic ethics is an eudemonistic one, which means that is it concerned with how we can live our lives in the best and happiest way possible. The virtues are a way to achieve that goal, a knowledge or a certain type of skill that we exercise in order to be in our very best behavior towards ourselves, others and nature or the divine. They thought virtues were the only path to happiness. As for misery, it was caused by the lack of rational thought usually inherent to sins or vices. Things that were neither virtuous or miserable were simply "indifferent" for the stoics, although they did admit some indifferent were more preferred than others. These indifferent things include a lot of stuff we would think to be central in our lives, like health, wealth or friends.

This stoic radicalism was a bit controversial in Antiquity, because most philosophers followed Aristotle, thinking a happy life was more than just virtue and required a bit of good fortune as well. For the stoics, however, only virtue could make or break happiness and only vices could breed unhappiness. So, if you had a terrible health and you were poor, you could only be deemed miserable by the stoics if you also acted in accordance to vices and not virtues, even if you considered your suffering to be very intense.

Another way in which the stoics differed from Aristotle is in the definition of virtue itself. While Aristotle defined virtue as a disposition to feel and act in a certain way, the stoics equated virtue with knowledge.

The first virtue, **practical wisdom**, is knowledge of what to do. **Temperance** is defined as knowledge of how much of a good thing to choose. **Justice** is the knowledge of the right distribution of goods to persons. **Courage** is the knowledge of what is terrible and what is not.

Although these virtues are quite similar to Plato's cardinal virtues, their interpretation is quite different. In this way, the stoics were innovators both in comparison to Plato and Aristotle in the way their understood virtuous behavior.

To live virtuously was to live according to the knowledge of all of nature, in complete accordance to the divine reason. A virtuous person must attempt to have a cosmic perspective of things, to realize what their place is in the world, their limitations and abilities.

To have a cosmic perspective means accepting that things happen for much bigger reasons and in accordance to a predetermined plan governed by nature's laws. It's ridiculous to cry over the death of a beloved friend or relative when such things happen in perfect harmony with the cosmos and when such events are not even categorized as important for happiness of unhappiness, they are in the group of indifferent we covered above.

The stoic virtues might be a bit difficult to understand, but many of them had sub-virtues to make it more explicit. We are now going to explain every virtue in detail:

PRACTICAL WISDOM

Practical wisdom is the knowledge of how to act and feel in the right way. This includes a few more abilities, mainly:

- Good sense

- Good calculation

- Quick wits

- Good sense of purpose (or discretion)

- Resourcefulness

As you can see, practical wisdom for the stoics is not only about acting in accordance to some moral code, it's thinking and practicing what you think in a distinct way. You need to learn how to think quickly, how to measure the context of our actions, how to find solutions in innovative ways and not making a fuss over everything. Practical wisdom involves some emotional intelligence and well as smart thinking abilities.

JUSTICE

We defined justice before as the knowledge of the right distributions of goods to persons, but this seems like an ancient formulation a bit difficult for us to understand. To make it simple, here are the other characteristics of a just person:

- Piety

- Honesty

- Equity

\-   Fair dealing

What this means is that a just person is also aware of his or hers standing in the universe and the respect owed to the divine. Like we have already covered, the laws governing humanity are as important as the laws of nature and have the same divine origin for the stoics, so they must always respect the gods in a pious manner.

A just stoic must also be honest and approach people with a good heart. He cannot be involved in trickery or deception and must always respect the principles of fair dealing.

Finally, a just stoic knows that all human beings are equal and their treatment should not be differentiated even though everyone has their own special characteristics, so a stoic must thrive to treat all people with equity.

COURAGE

We previously defined courage as the knowledge of what is terrible and what is not, which can be translated as the ability to recognize what we should be fearful of and what we shouldn't be. For the stoics, a courageous person has the following characteristics:

- Endurance

- Confidence

- High-mindedness

- Cheerfulness

- Industriousness

These might be surprising, unless you understand that most of stoic courage has most to do with fortitude, rather than our traditional understanding of courage. Fortitude basically means that you are not deterred from difficulty, it does not mean you seek to put yourself in dangerous situations or conquer your fears when they are indifferent to you. That is why a stoic must be capable of enduring hard situations with confidence and cheerfulness. It also explains why being high-minded, or having an upright moral character, and having a love for work (industriousness) are important for a courageous stoic, since all of these characteristic make up for a determined person capable of overcoming any sort of challenge.

TEMPERANCE

Temperance is another way for moderation, and we had defined it as the knowledge of how much of a good thing to choose, meaning, knowing when to stop. The characteristic of a moderate person are:

- Good discipline

- Seemliness

- Modesty

- Self-control

These virtues might be more reminiscent of our traditional view of the stoic. Indeed, in order for someone to follow the stoic philosophy with its emphasis on the cosmic view of the world and reality, discipline is important. In order for us to practice our virtues, we must also have self-control, so we are not controlled by our emotions. Modesty is to keep us from being delusional, particularly because it might interfere with our piety. And seemliness is important for organized logical thinking, which will lead us to make rational decisions.

Having just presented you with the stoic virtues, I think it's useful for us to also understand the stoic vices. These are: ignorance, injustice, cowardice and wantonness, the very opposites of the virtues. The stoics considered virtues to be very central in life, and forming indeed the cornerstone of happiness and therefore being the root of their entire ethical system. Developing this virtues could shake your emotional and rational life completely, leading you not only to act but think differently. Virtues can be potentially attained by every human beings - another controversial idea, since in Antiquity many virtues were thought to be innate. The stoics do not let you go that easily and remind you that you too, as well as any other person, can begin to develop and cherish these virtues in your everyday life.

To end this section, I will share you with a beautiful passage of the *Meditations*, the book by our favorite Roman Emperor Marcus Aurelius containing his most private thoughts:

"If someone is able to show me that what I think or do is not right, I will happily change, for I seek the truth, by which no one was ever truly harmed. It is the person who continues in his self-deception and ignorance who is harmed."

It's high time for us to follow his advice and start changing ourselves too. When we refuse to see the light of reason, we are the main victims of our self-deception.

Chapter 3: Stoicism and Religious Parallels

As we have covered before, stoicism has had some influence over Christian religion and has overall many religious parallels. This section is devoted to exploring the nature of those parallels.

The most important parallel is probably the concept of *askesis*. This word has been connected with the term asceticism, but actually askesis really means the practice or training of the self. It is a core belief of the stoics that we can train ourselves to be better, mainly by practicing the virtues and by restraining negative emotions interfere with our judgment. Likewise, askesis is a cornerstone of many religions. With Christianity, it evolved to become the world asceticism, a training of the self indeed but devoid of "sinful" aspects, that were terrible in Christian eyes but indifferent for the stoics.

For both Christians and stoics, and even more for Muslims or Jews, the devotion to God and living in accordance to the divine plan requires a lot of self-discipline. Think about the forbidden foods for both Muslims and Jews, for example, or the strict chastity of Christianity. For Stoics, the major thing was to practice the virtues without extremes and living with a global perspective, cultivating the necessary knowledge to be in tune with divinity.

It's interesting to note most monotheistic religions also share the cosmopolitans and egalitarians concepts of stoicism. The City of God of Christianity is similar to the cosmopolitan beliefs of the Stoics, who thought proper government was always possible by applying God's laws. There is some downside to this however, since stoic philosophers were huge fans of absolute monarchies. Even though the absolute monarch was thought as the plenitude of the four virtues and an agent of the divine, it this inspire the Divine Right Theory which allowed the kings of the Middle Ages to proclaim a divine right to rule everywhere in the Christian world. Still, we find echoes of this in other major religions - weren't Moses or Mohammed holy monarchs as well?

Similarly, the concepts of quiet piety are important in all major religions. Even though many have advices of common rituals of devotion, they still consider faith to be a very personal thing. The stoics also thought that the divine could be found within through quiet reflection, and they weren't big fans of piety as a badge of good behavior. Most religions tell people to be modest and to practice their faith for themselves, not for others to see. To give charity only for the pictures and not when there are no eyes to see it, that is not the religious or Stoic ideal.

But the major common ground between Stoicism and religion is probably how it deals with hurtful events. For Stoics and religious people, even the worst pain possible must have a reason, be a part of a larger plan. You'll see people taking comfort in religion after traumatic events because it provides a sense of logic and stability, it soothes the most extreme emotions of distress and tells them everything that happens has a cause and that reality is governed by divinely sanctioned laws.

For both Christianity and stoicism, for example, God equates with the logo, the internal logic of things, the infinite mind that rules the universe. Although Christian folktales have transformed the image of God into a bearded man that lives in the sky, we can say this is the downgraded picture for the masses to have something concrete to worship. For the Middle Age philosophers who constructed the entire Christian theology with Greek inspiration, God has a lot more in common with the pneuma, for example.

The logos is understood as God's will and for both Christian and Stoics, you can't really expect God to do you some good just because He feels like it. God gave a set of rules and advices to follow, simply principles ruling the universe and even some virtues to help you navigate life and pointed out some vices so you won't be tempted into being miserable. Yet, some people still do not follow God's will. They do not respected the logos and act irrationally. The Christian god is much more forgiving, however, than the logos of the Stoics, a blind principle of creation who is not interested in daily matters. But for the Christians, God's intervention is so rare it is called a miracle - in most cases, what you should do is follow God's will and expect nothing in return, except for the proper working of the universe that should benefit everyone in the end.

Both Christians and Stoics also believe that if you follow God's will, cultivate the cardinal virtues, avoid the vices, and attempt to have a global, cosmic perspective of things, you will be happy. It is, in fact, the only path to happiness.

Indeed, in ethical terms, there's much to draw from both Stoicism and Christianity, which shows how much influence this philosophy had on the early days of the Church. Both believed that enduring hardships can have a positive outcome on your character, mostly because it teaches you how to live in accordance to virtues and to have a harder grip on the reality of the world. If you suffer, you will be drawn to self-reflection, you will ponder and wonder, you will be forced to find solutions to unanswerable questions. In short, hardships draw you closer to God's plan, because you are forced to contemplate it due to the circumstances.

Stoics and Christians are also highly vigilant of the innate depravity of men. Since both systems of thought think virtue is ultimately dependent on the individual, there is also a choice to be made and many people make the wrong one. The raw, natural state of mankind isn't something neither stoics of Christians admire - there's too much lust, impulsion, irrationality. Men should be tamed with thought, careful examination, self-discipline. There's too much about mankind that is not innate, it is only in a potential state because we are all rational creatures. But you need to be guided to become truly rational, and that transformation always involves a recognition of the role both God and the universe play in your life as it is.

As philosophies that loathe men in its "natural" state, both Stoicism and Christianity absolutely hate excesses. Although there might be some disagreements with Aristotle's concept of the Golden Mean is a highly appreciated one by both Stoicism and Christianity. Both stoicism and

Christianity also disliked the fixation on material wealth and instead argued that one is only truly wealthy when he is satisfied and grateful for what he already has - if he think he owns too much, the virtuous thing to do is to share or give away. Both also disliked greed, even if Seneca sometimes tried to find justifications for it.

Finally, both also believed that true peace could only be found by detaching oneself from the world. This doesn't mean a Stoic or Christian shouldn't be involved in worldly matters, such as standing up in the face of injustice, but they shouldn't consider it the end all be all. Instead, they should focus on the inner world and self-reflex ion above all things, they should cherish the inner connection to the divine and not be distracted all the time by the outside world. There is a certain difference, however. Christians dream about the kingdom of God in the afterlife, while Stoics accept the fact the logic of the world is beyond them and everything that happens is not for them to control - they can only control themselves, and that is more than enough work.

Interestingly, there's another world religion that can be easily compared with Stoicism, for they share many of the same beliefs and intuitions regarding the universe and how human beings should relate to it. They both believe that all kinds of happiness must come from within, that they are part of an internal process of self-examination and self-control of your emotions and desires.

Buddhism aims to liberate human beings from suffering, while Stoics aim to be happy in harmony with the divine principles that rule the universe. They take a similar path getting there, because it always has to do with the way you relate to the outside reality and how little you hope it to change. Both philosophies urge you, in turn, to change yourself, to build resilience and let go of outside yearnings, especially those relating to material things.

Buddhism was also lead by a powerful man, since Siddhartha was thought to be originally a prince that gave up all his luxuries and powers to meditate upon the existence of human beings and find the ultimate truth that would liberate them from suffering. Even though Marcus Aurelius does not have the same history and chose not to give anything away, but rather face his responsibilities with determination and diligence, it is still interesting to note how two virtuous and powerful men of the Ancient World were concerned about the plagues of human existence and how to fix them

Buddhism also believes that the universe has an internal logic and that the divine is everywhere, making a strict distinction between the mind and the material world. Likewise, Stoics metaphysics, as we have seen, sees men as being composed of mind and body, even though they admit that everything is material - because the material is divine, nonetheless.

Both philosophies are also very pragmatic and practical, embodying effective lifestyles for the practitioners who adhere to these systems of thought. Perhaps the popularity of Buddhism in the Western world would subside if Stoicism was presented in the same terms and if their rituals and habits were systematized to become real classes on building resilience and a strong core.

Chapter 4: In Control of your emotions, not situation

Most people will think stoics hate emotions. The reality is slightly more complex. For Stoics, emotions are not important in the sense they cannot be the justification for behaviors. If you are having a terrible day and you let feelings get the best of you, you might be rather unpleasant for loved ones trying to help. For the Stoics, that is not an acceptable behavior. The cardinal virtues should always guide you in your relationships towards others, the universe and yourself, no matter how much you might be suffering or the emotional distress you could be feeling.

Now, that does not mean the Stoics thought all emotions were the same. In fact, they did encourage at least some emotions. There is a stoic list of the three good feelings, in opposition to the three bad passions - the word passion in the Ancient World had a far more negative sense than in modernity, being equated with irrationality and excessive behavior.

The three good feelings were: Joy, Wish and Caution. The three passions in opposition were Pleasure, Appetite and Fear, all three being excesses of the three good feelings. The passion of distress didn't have any matching good feeling, it was just bad pure and simple.

Each of these passions could lead to specific bad events or emotions. Take appetite, for example. If you are greedy, it means you have a great appetite for money, and if you are a glutton or an alcoholic, it means you have a great appetite for food and drinks. For the Stoics, wasting your life away wanting to take more and more things, especially when you couldn't have them, was an immoral waste of time. When people feel an appetite, they convince themselves their life is worthless if they cannot have the next fix. Often, they don't even enjoy that piece of cake or that cocktail, they need it like a thirsty man needs water. It becomes a nuisance, an obligation. It becomes something that controls you, instead of you being in control. And your entire mental stability is dependent on an appetite, which is a degrading way to live.

So, in order to avoid the negative outcomes of appetite but knowing human beings are always going to be desiring something, the Stoics tell you not to have an appetite, but a wish. Wishes are things we know may not come true, so we can easily life without. I can wish for a perfect piece of chocolate cake right now, but my life doesn't depend on it. It would be great sure, and very pleasurable, but it's not my goal or my priority and I can easily function without it. It's like an extra. In a way, Stoicism tells you to turn all your appetites into nice extras, so you can learn to enjoy them more and consume them in moderation.

I might want a fancier car or a better TV, but I am not taking a second job just because of that. I'm not taking time away from myself or my family due to material appetites. Instead, I'll keep work diligently, acting my best, and if I get a promotion in the end of the year, only then will I consider buying the material things I wish. I'm fine without them and will continue to be, even if I never get that promotion that allows me to become more wealthy and spend more money on stuff.

Wishing is a form of detachment. You can still be wise and logical even when you are wishing something, in fact, as we saw in the example above, it can even be an extra form of motivation to cultivate the virtues. But you know in your heart it isn't the core of the world, and so you'll never give it a second thought in case your wish does not come true.

Then, let us consider the opposition between Joy and Pleasure. Joy is the contentment of the present, a carpe diem sort of feeling. You look at your life from a global perspective and you realize just how happy you are. You might not love your job, but you love your family and it is a great achievement you are able to provide for them. You might not have found someone to share your life with, but you have a great group of friends who will be there for you no matter what. You have all your basic needs fulfilled and still have time and energy to devote yourself to other hobbies that make you happy. Overall, and considering the state of the world, don't you have just a bunch of things to be grateful for?

Now compare that blissful feeling to pleasure. Pleasure is crude, carnal. You just had a one night stand, let's say, and yet there you are looking at other women again, working the bars to see if you can find another partner for tonight. You are so focused on future pleasure you cannot even appreciate what you have at this moment. You envision a version of you that is so much wealthier, happier, better-looking, that the entire view you hold of yourself and your life is distorted. When you do achieve a pleasurable moment, you try to hold on to it. Imagine you are going out with your friends for the first time in a while, you're having loads of fun, so you can't stop yourself from overdoing it and spend the rest of the night puking. In that case, you were driven the pleasure not joy, you weren't really content because you kept thinking you could have more and more fun, until it made you sick.

Since stoics know you cannot control reality, they do not look for sources of even more instability. Pining for something and overdoing pleasurable activities is becoming too reliant on outsider stimuli, you lose the ability to think for yourself and make pondered, rational decisions.

You break your self-discipline and become a puppet of emotions, someone who cannot be trusted and who will attempt any kind of self-justification without owning up to his or hers mistakes.

Now, let us consider the last opposition. When we are cautious, it means we are well-prepared for hardship, we are resilient. If you know from the start some things are just out of your control, you won't be so disappointed when they turn out in a bad way. You might want that beautiful girl to marry you, but you know your life goals differ and there's a good chance she'll say no. Still, you ask, wishing but calmly accepting the worst possible outcome.

If you had let fear dominate you, you wouldn't even wish in the first place. You'd pace around your room, creating alternative scenarios in your head. You'd waste valuable time and energy without coming up with any solution, without the will to face reality and too frightened to settle the issue once and for all. Eventually, your lack of initiative could lead to the break-up and that would be the end.

You see, fear is actually the very irrational emotion that worrying deeply about things you cannot control will somehow make them better. You might suffer about the afterlife, what happens when we die, how you will die and so on and so forth, and become completely immobilized due to your fears. Even if you can be joyful and practice wish instead of appetite, if you are fearful everything is worthless, because you'll just spend all your joyful moments thinking that they will soon end. What's the point of such things? There is none, and that is what the stoics try to tell you over and over.

We've mentioned the self-discipline of the stoics over and over but still haven't provided you with any practical examples. Since the point of this section is to teach you how to be in control of your emotions, not the situation, here are some exercises straight from Antiquity and the likes of Marcus Aurelius, Epictetus and Seneca:

#1 EXERCISE: A VIEW FROM ABOVE

I think we've covered the importance of this in many earlier sections. From the cover view of Stoic metaphysics to the religious parallels or the importance of virtues such as piety, much of Stoic philosophy aims to make you realize how much of your life you owe to the laws of the universe and how you are but a tiny bit of the cosmos, with no particular importance.

What this exercise demands you do is taking that thought one step further and turn it into some sort of meditation. Close your eyes and envision yourself in the third person, an image of you just sitting exactly where you are now. Then, slowly, start zooming out. Think of your sister, wife, parent, roommate in the next division, taking care of their own affairs. Then think about your neighbors, the people inhabiting the building you live in. Then, the city, the country, the continent, planet Earth, our galaxy...you'll slowly begin to discover just how little you are, how trivial your concerns and how irrelevant your suffering. Why bother with a humiliation you suffered at work or school, for example, if your bullies are also just as small as you? Why waste your precious time on this Earth concerning yourself with meaningless stuff, instead of focusing in learning the correct path, the Will of the logos?

This humbling exercise was followed by none other than Marcus Aurelius, the most powerful man of the universe in his day. Surprising to think a Roman Emperor actually took time out from his incredibly busy days to convince himself his endeavors did not matter in the large scale and that he should also remind himself of how irrelevant he was, even if everyone around him treated him like God made flesh. Think of this interesting quote of his regarding failure: "Is it your reputation that is bothering you? But look at how soon we're all forgotten. The abyss of endless time that swallows all. The emptiness of all those applauding hands."

2 Negative visualization

Negative visualization is a fancy term for picturing the worst possible outcome, the worst case scenario, preparing yourself for disappointment before you even know the answer. Why should you cause yourself to be unhappy in such a fashion? Actually, the goal is precisely the opposite. By constantly envisioning how things could be different and more difficult, you should slowly begin to appreciate the goodness in your life.

This simple exercise gives you fortitude and resilience with which to face your challenges in life. It lets you detach from the most painful events, because you already knew beforehand they could end like this or because you know in your heart there is still plenty to be thankful for. Imagine you must bury your father and his death makes you miserable. At least your relationship with your father was something to be cherished, the sort of thing you will always take with you in life, the basis of your character. Many people aren't given the chance to have such a relationship with neither of their parents, so you should be thankful to be in this much pain - it meant you were incredibly happy and lucky before.

Obviously, you are not supposed to spend all your days obsessing over terrible things happening. It's more like stuff you should have in the back of your head to give you a real sense of things.

By realizing how much things can change from one moment to the next, always having the worst case scenario in the back of your mind, you'll also be much better trained to enjoy the present. Because you know everything is transient, you'll need to be carpe diem all the way if you ever want to experience joy. You'll also become a much more grateful person, the sort of individual that understand how lucky he is and because of that bears no ill-will towards the unfortunate ones that are still struggling to survive.

Negative visualization is a cure against vanity and greed. By practicing this simple technique, you will become calmer and more relaxed, in tune with the universe and capable of feeling grateful even when it seems your entire life is going in a downright spiral.

#4 Philanthropy

Nowadays, we usually take philanthropy to mean giving lots and lots of money to charity, becoming famous and having a library or a dorm named after you. Well, that's obviously not the whole story. Everyone can be a philanthropist because, in its origin, it just means doing things for the common good, for the wellbeing of your society or community.

Since Stoicism has always been a philosophy closely connected to worldly affairs and politics, it's natural to see the role philanthropy plays. When you act in a generous way, you are exercising your best virtues, becoming increasingly confident and certain of yourself. On the other hand, it means you are doing your part in creating the cosmopolitan brotherhood of men, contributing to the common good and making sure society will be governed by divine laws of equality.

#5 Voluntary discomfort

Voluntary discomfort is a hard one, which many people might feel reluctant about trying. An exercise suggested by Epictetus, the Slave, it basically advises you to put yourself in uncomfortable or downright painful situations to build up some resilience to hardship. These exercises might include sleeping without a pillow or a mattress, fasting, taking cold showers, going out in a snowy night without a coat, not taking painkillers for an injury, and so on and so forth. It seems like a rather masochistic thing to do, yet many professions in law enforcement and military do the exact same thing.

The point of this exercise is for you to understand that comfort is a relative term and you can indeed survive without any comfort at all. You will learn to cherish the comfort you have, but you'll know how to live without it. You slowly become increasingly independent from exterior things and learn to trust only in your survival skills, which you can take with you anywhere and that form the basis of your character.

#6 Contemplate the actions of the Stoic Sage

The Stoic Sage isn't a real person. It's an ideal man or woman, the sort of person every stoics wishes to become, yet there is always something that damages our moral certitude. Whenever something happens, just think to yourself - what would the Stoic Sage do? This harmonious creature of our imagination acts as a way to remind ourselves it is always possible to do better.

Are you going through a rough patch and you have no idea of how to handle a situation? Well, if you were the Stoic Sage what would you do? Would you run away cowardly or face and conquer your fears? The Stoic Sage is like a cheat code, a way for you to always know the answer. Someone who can gather all the cardinal virtues and act in accordance to the laws of divine nature, here's who you have to look up to and attempt to imitate. Even if it is such a figment of your imagination, it shows you how you do have the creativity and moral compass to at least make the hypothetical good decision or action. If the Stoic Sage exists within you, it means your emotions still haven't got completely hold of you and you still have the chance to control yourself, no matter the situation you might be facing.

#7 Learn to love your fate

Amor fate is a Latin phrase that relates to the love of fate. This was very important for the Stoics. If you love your fate, which can be translated as loving your life, you will be in acceptance of everything that happens to you. You will understand that you are not in control but that is does not matter, as long as you can still find solace and happiness and things to be grateful for. Your fate might have deviated you from your initial childhood dreams, but look where it took you, what characteristics such detour forced you to develop, what things you have discovered that you never even imagine to be possible. Remind yourself that each individual has a purpose and that is what you should be striving for, even if you are not quite sure of what it is, is the best way to learn to love your fate.

There is a famous passage from the Meditations of Marcus Aurelius that sums up basically everything we have covered in this section. Due to its beauty and relevance, here it is in its integrity. Marcus

Aurelius was an accomplished writer, so you'll see it's worth reading all the way through:

"Constantly reflect on how swiftly all that exists and is coming to be is swept past us and disappears from sight. For substance is like a river in perpetual flow, and its activities are ever changing, and its causes infinite in their variations, and hardly anything at all stands still; and ever at our side is the immeasurable span of the past and the yawning gulf of the future, into which all things vanish away. Then how is he not a fool who in the midst of all this is puffed up with pride, or tormented, or bewails his lot as though his troubles will endure for any great while?"

Chapter 5: Misconceptions of Stoicism

Now that we've covered what stoicism is, let's talk about what it isn't. Sometimes, because stoicism is considered a philosophy of the "tough", certain elements get misinterpreted and create entirely new ideas from thin air. Here's a basic list about what stoicism isn't for you to remember whenever someone try to fool you:

Stoicism is not a religion or a cult

You do not "join" stoicism. It is not a club. It is also not an organized religion or a religious cult, you do not have to change your live entirely or adhere to a specific dress code or code of conduct. Stoicism is a philosophy, a way to think about the world that may or may not affect your actions and choices. It is a system, but not a system of religious belief - in fact, you can practice many of the stoic principles while being an atheist. As a philosophy, stoicism should lead you to further inquiry, it is not an open and shut book that will give you all the answers. There is nothing worse than mistaking a philosophy for ideology - keep re-thinking your stoicism and make it better by constant questioning.

Many people throughout history have tried to join stoicism and religion together. Although there are parallels, as we have mentioned before, they should not be mistaken, and stoicism should maintain its intellectual integrity and freedom.

Stoicism is not for the cold-hearted

Just because stoicism urges you to control - not negate - your emotions, it does not mean you stop feeling stuff just because you want to live by stoic principles. Stoicism is about self-control and self-discipline, and it is very telling that many people in today's world will immediately equate that with cold-heartedness. Not being controlled by your passions, sadness's or rage fits means you are capable to make rational choices and can see reality more clearly. Even if some people are more prone to control and discipline than others, everything in life requires some degree of emotion-control. If you have children, for example, you might find yourself almost pulling your hair out but you do not act on those strange desires, because you know them to be irrational and that the up bring of your children in a healthy and loving home should be your priority. Likewise, many professions are time consuming and incredibly stressful, dealing with dramatic situations on a daily basis. Health professionals, emergency workers, rescue mission operators, even psychologists or teachers realize that they must assume a professional attitude of self-control at all times, or they risk putting themselves and other people in bad positions.

Most importantly, though, stoicism does not want you to stop feeling positive emotions. If you are thrilled by music and think that reading a good book is a pleasurable exercise, continue doing so. If you are interested in the problems of your fellow men and want to better their lives, you shouldn't force that empathy out of your system. But acting in the heat of the moment can lead to more wrongdoing - after all, as people say, the road to hell is paved with good intentions.

Stoics are not pessimists or fatalists

People tend to see determinism as fatalism in disguise. All determinism tells you is that events have causes and that reality unfolds as an infinite sequel of cause and effect. Fatalism, on the other hand, tells you that everything is going to happen in a certain way no matter what you do about it, so you might as well do nothing.

Stoicism, with its strong emphasis on ethics, could never accept such a proposition. For stoicism, there is still some causality linked to human agency, meaning your choices and decisions can make or break the unfolding of a whole new sequel of events. You can choose what to do, what not to do, what to say and what not to say. You can decide when you should stand up for yourself and others or cowardly walk away. Most importantly, you can decide to better yourself and to manage your emotions, you can choose to be a stoic and act rationally.

Yes, there is causes in the universe beyond your understanding and you might just be playing a part in a huge play of the cosmos. But you still do not know the lines, you are making them up as you go, so you might as well make them up properly and logically and strive to be the best version of yourself that is humanly possible.

The stoic advice about imagining the worst possible scenario is also not a call for pessimism. Quite the opposite - what you are supposed to do is to imagine the various different ways in which your life could be terrible, in which you could be unhappy, so you can fully appreciate what was given to you. Stoics are not pessimists, they are realists. They hate self-pity, so they make themselves aware of how truly bad things could be in order to protect themselves from disillusionment. If you are constantly reminding yourself of how things could be different and that your decisions might not have the positive outcome you so desire, you are controlling your emotions in advance, shielding yourself from great pain and disappointment.

But you shouldn't obsess over it. Doing so is wallowing in fear and self-pity, not stoic attitudes to take at all. To think rationally and logically about the world is to ponder the several causations that can lead to a negative or positive outcome and prepare yourself mentally to both. If everything succeeds, you don't let it go to your head; if everything falls apart, you don't despair. Stoicism, as the prime philosophy of self-discipline, self-perfection and self-awareness, teaches you to be better than this.

Stoicism is not a how-to-guide for denial

Stoicism teaches you to deal with reality, it does not teach you about escaping it. If you avoid confrontation or if you feign ignorance or indifference towards your surroundings, you are not being a stoic, you are just becoming alienated. Many stoics, as we've seen, were accomplished politicians, valuable members of society and committed citizens. They knew how to manage their emotions in order to make rational decisions, but they did not regard the evils of the world as unsolvable. True, many things are not under your control, but many others are, and you shouldn't use stoicism as an excuse for inaction. You don't shrug your shoulders, look around and say: oh well, it's always been this way. Instead, you own your life and carefully examine what you can improve and what you should accept.

Stoicism cannot become a pleasant lie you tell yourself whenever life gets hard. If you want that job, that relationship, that friendship or project to succeed, you will have to rationally measure how much is under your control and what you can achieve through hard work. An unrequited love is something you should forget about, while a stale yet loving marriage might still be worth saving. Often, people confuse the stoic mindset with indifference, betraying a historical and complex philosophical system in the process. Indifference leads you to inaction, while stoicism should be as practical as possible, leading you to try new solutions and ask new questions about your problems and ills in life. With its focus on universality, it should also inspire you to work along your fellow men to better the world you all are living in.

Chapter 6: Peace of Mind

What does it truly mean to be a stoic? We've covered many of the main concepts here already but here is a central one left, directly connected with the stoic notion of happiness.

After all, we've been mentioning again and again that living virtuously leads to happiness and happiness is following the law of nature, in a rather circular argument. But what does Stoic happiness feels like, since there are so many forbidden emotions? Most people never really define what happiness feels like, they just define their causes or consequences. Like: if I am happy I smile, or, this new promotion makes me happy, that new relationship, that pile of money. You'll notice I've only listed transient things, the kind of stuff most stoics are deeply suspicious off. But is stoic happiness also a transient thing, even with all the exercises offered by ancient Stoics? Let us find out. The concept of Apathies, or peace of mind, was the stuff of dreams for the stoics. It was all they ever longed for in life, the perpetual state in which the Stoic Sage was imagined as living in.

In short, apatheia simply means not being haunted by passions. It's an a-passionate state, in which complicated emotions are not constantly tormenting you and mixing up your every thought. Even though it sounds easy, we've seen how hard it can be to be completely free from all kinds of passions and how hard it is to cultivate the right set of virtues and control your feelings so you'll only experience three recommended emotions.

The peace of mind achieved through the control of the passions was the goal of the Stoic exercises we covered in the previous session. All of that daily hard work was meant to achieve this particular and quiet form of freedom, a lifestyle of serenity that was not dissociated from civic engagement, joy and gratefulness.

There was another school of thought in Ancient Greek philosophy that also advocated for a freedom from the passions, albeit in a slightly different way. Perhaps by comparing the two you'll be able to understand the singularity of apatheia.

The Epicurists used the term ataraxia to describe a person who was free from troubles and worries. A philosophy of happiness by moderation,

Epicurismwas also very popular during Ancient times and continues to be until this day. You might think ataraxia is similar to apatheia, but there is one major difference: while ataraxia and Epicurist philosophy as a whole admonishes you to retreat from everyday life and focus on moderate pleasures, the Stoics still urge you to engage, to be a philanthropist, to realise how lucky you are and be a cosmopolitan.

Apatheia is about controlling your emotions through a rational lens. If you are sure of the principles of stoicism, virtue and nature, you will quietly understand most of your distress is without reason. Your wrath towards someone who wronged you or annoying people you find in your daily life is useless, particularly because most vice is caused simply by ignorance. If you want to be virtuous and have peace of mind, why not try to teach others the rightful path instead of running away?

Even though many people equate apatheia with the image of the quiet sage that sits pondering about the world on top of a mountain, you should still remember that apatheia is a concept of an extremely practical philosophy based on ethics.

This means apatheia could never lead you towards inaction, but rather towards a self-perfect way to act in the world, refrained from passions and informed by logic and piety.

However, it is true apatheia is mostly connected to thinking and inner life and not so much to the outside world. The stoics knew there were some thinking habits that must be cherished in order for apatheia to be maintained. Here are a few, that you can combine with the stoic exercises for optimal Stoicism:

#1 Constantly self-examine and be brutally honest with yourself

If you engage in self-deception, there is no way you will be able to change yourself and turn into a virtuous person. Whenever you meditate over the things that happened in a given day or past actions, recognize your flaws and mistakes and look for a cause and a solution. If you acted aggressively because you were jealous, what made you act that way? Was it a deep-seated lack of self-confidence? Was it a lack of trust between yourself and a loved one due to past occurrences you rather not dwell on too much? What about your own personal failures, are all of them the fault of your parents, your teachers, your boss, the weather? When you are capable of looking yourself in the eyes and saying: I failed, but will do better next time, you will have the peace of mind to really try again and not be tormented by ghosts of your past errors.

#2 Educate yourself and turn thoughts into action

A stoic should always aim for more knowledge, so you shouldn't ever stop educating yourself. But reading books and discussing them intelligently with like-minded people is not enough, you need to actually put those thoughts into action. If you are aware of all the stoic principles, but you do not have the guts to live by them, what good does it do? Likewise, if after educating yourself about a certain practice or attitude, you continue to display and abide by it, you are not being truthful to yourself and making the best of the knowledge you have acquired over time.

Many people are fine when it comes to reading and pretending to know more a subject than what they really know, but fewer and fewer actually attempt to live by the things they learn along the way.

#3 Retreat into yourself

The outside world is a confusing thing full of triggers of distress. Every now and again, it's important to retreat into yourself and really dig deep to understand why you must be feeling a certain way and how to change it. In order to feel a real tranquility of mind, you must cherish it and nourish it, delve in the depths of your thoughts and let yourself be lost in your train of thinking. Some people might prefer trying some meditation exercises to really let go of the outside world and focus on their inner selves. After a busy day when you hardly have time to stop, it's important to relax. But relaxing without resorting to entertainment, but a different kind of relaxation where the goal is to develop some degree of intimacy with your own mind. After all, you'll never be able to really change if you don't know yourself.

Chapter 7: Daily living as a Stoic

Now we've arrived at the most important part of this book. Sure, it is interesting to know about stoic principles and understand the history behind them, but what's that for if you can't live as a stoic? For most people in the XXI century, the stoic metaphysics might seem flawed and something akin to a fairytale. But is it the same case when we talk about stoic ethics? I don't think so.

Stoic ethics is a complex and fascinating system of action that allows us to better ourselves and live in an engaged way. You'll be wrong to think it is a system of the past, since it is becoming more and more relevant. In a culture of consumption and capitalism, where people are inspired to look at ourselves and others as mere tools of material wealth, and in a culture where comfort and lack of risk seems to dominate, how can we possibly find meaning?

The meaning of life has been the most important theme in philosophy. The stoics tell us that we should live in accordance to nature and we shouldn't deviate from that path, we shouldn't expect nature to change for our sakes but it is our responsibility to change ourselves and our perspective to match that of reality.

In this chapter, I will present you to a series of quotes from famous Stoics and explain how to apply them in your daily life. I prefer you read the original quotes so you can tell how meaningful they still are, after almost 2000 years, and so you will have a first contact with the writings of glorious stoic philosophers. People like Epictetus or Marcus Aurelius wanted their principles to guide their action, so they were incredibly concrete in their advices. You'll find here quotes to guide through the daily interaction with your co-workers, your relationships, the political system of your country, religion and love. We'll discover the stoic principles together through the words of the people who formed them and who lived by them, even when it was extremely hard to do so.

How to deal with people

The majority of the distress we feel does not come from existential angst, but from our dealings with other people. We find relationships to be a hard thing to navigate and we are constantly wondering about the right course of action. Other people can awaken the worst or the best in you, depending on how wisely you choose your friends. And they can anger and upset you damaging the tranquility of your mind.

The Stoics were people engaged in political life, so they were acutely aware of how difficult it can be to manage personal relationships in a satisfactory way. That's why so many of them wrote extensively about it, using it as a sort of test of self-control much more efficient than calamities or poverty. Here are some useful thoughts about how to be Stoic in daily life when dealing with the people around you:

"Any person capable of angering you becomes your master;

he can anger you only when you permit yourself to be disturbed by him." Epictetus

Epictetus was a former slave, so he probably had a fair share of assholes to deal with during his lifetime. He wasn't considered to be a proper human being until he earned his freedom, so we was constantly put down by the people around him who considered themselves to be superior.

The way he found to deal with this constant annoyance was to simply ignore it. If someone is trying to make up mad, why are you making their wishes come true? Why are you letting our well-being be controlled by someone else?

Even though this might be easier said than done, it's still quite baffling the way in which most people will spend hours obsessing over an exchange of heated words or an insult. If someone calls you an idiot and you aren't one, why did you get so upset? It's their own opinion and it's completely worthless to you.

With so much talk about building resistance and being in control of your own emotions, it would ridiculous if a Stoic would let himself be disturbed by another person just because of anger. If you let a person know you won't be bothered with their silly criticism you are making them understand their anger is beneath you and that the only proper way to communicate is with an honest and courageous conversation and exchange of views.

"When you wake up in the morning, tell yourself: the people I deal with today will be meddling, ungrateful, arrogant, dishonest, jealous and surly. They are like this because they can't tell good from evil. But I have seen the beauty of good, and the ugliness of evil, and have recognized that the wrongdoer has a nature related to my own - not of the same blood and birth, but the same mind, and possessing a share of the divine. And so none of them can hurt me. No one can implicate me in ugliness. Nor can I feel angry at my relative, or hate him. We were born to work together like feet, hands and eyes, like the two rows of teeth, upper and lower. To obstruct each other is unnatural. To feel anger at someone, to turn your back on him: these are unnatural." Marcus Aurelius

This is long quote from Marcus Aurelius but an important one - we suggest you frame it and gaze at it constantly during the holidays, to keep you from smothering your loved ones when they start getting annoying.

Now, seriously - most of us have to navigate daily life with a bunch of company we may dislike. You might hate your sister or your boss, you might want to murder half of the metro or bus passengers during your commute, or call the police on your neighbors when they keep making noise at three in the morning.

The best way to make peace with the amount of negative stimulus coming from the dealing with fellow human beings is to understand you are all the same, deep down. And if some of them might be angrier or more impolite, a lot of that is due to a lack of knowledge or education, to a flaw in character that does not change their nature and their position as fellow members of the human race, equally worthy of respect and human rights.

When you respond to an unpleasant person in an equally unpleasant way, you are presenting yourself as being equally impolite. You aren't being a good example or even a good member of the community, but simply put, you're acting as just another asshole who is ruin someone else's day.

The best way to be a Stoic is to prove yourself above such basic feelings and be in control of your emotions. You can deal with an unpleasant person, after all, you've been fostering enough discipline to let you live through the worst calamities, but you can't be cold in the face of an insult during your morning commute? Most people are simply trying to survive, and not all of them have had the same privileges than you. Those who had and maybe even more but still cannot behave properly are to be pitied and not loathed, because you've seen much worse things and you know there's always a way to turn around and start fresh.

Being a Stoic is being in control of yourself even in the face of the worst kind of people. So don't let them ruin your balance, strive to be the better man and show them what proper behavior looks like at all times.

Most importantly, be empathetic towards those whose lives have been so rough that they don't know how to act any better. Sometimes a little understanding and respect is all people are asking for and it's something that comes free of charge.

"Withdraw into yourself, as far as you can. Associate with those who will make a better man of you. Welcome those whom you yourself can improve. The process is mutual; for men learn while they teach." Seneca

You yourself are your best friend and will remain so for the rest of your life. That might be a bitter truth, but it's still the truth. When it comes to choosing friends, you must choose them carefully to make sure you are surrounded with people who will make the best of you come to the surface and not the worst.

Often, those who live in bad company feel depressed and miserable, thinking there's no way to turn their life around. It's no wonder, if you only have bad example surrounding you, there's less will to become better.

However, when you choose your friends wisely, you'll notice a wonderful process taking place. Not only will you feel much better about yourself and have much more determination to better your flaws, you will learn from your experiences and from those around you. When you are discussing an issue that worries you, talking about it with someone else will make your ideas become clearer, even when you disagree.

Most people learn while they teach, meaning, they become wiser when they share their ideas with others. If you want to make the best of life, make sure to always have a good friend on speed-dial, someone you can call whenever you want to talk about the stuff that haunts your mind who can clear your thoughts and make them more logical and less threatening.

Even though, in the end, you can only really count on yourself, in this brotherhood of men we are all going through the same scary process of living and it is important for us to share our experiences in order to grow and improve our societies.

How to look at wealth

Worrying about wealth is simply a part of the human existence. We crave several things, some of which we desperately need for survive, some of which exist merely to entertain us and make existence a little bit more comfortable. Since many of the stoics were either super rich or super poor, they knew how important wealth is. Because most of them lived in the Roman society, a place obsessed with status, gold and honor, they wrote about the interaction between these three spheres. Still, many of their advices still apply in the XXI century, since we ourselves are obsessed with wealth in a capitalist society. Here are some thoughts on wealth and why it does not matter as much as you think it does:

"Wealth consists not in having great possessions, but in having few wants." Epictetus

Spoken as a true slave, we could say. As someone who grew up having no material possessions to call its own, Epictetus learned how to live depending on other things for happiness. He understood at an early age that most wealthy people are constantly yearning for something else- more houses, more power, more prestige, more clothes, more gold...they simply cannot be satisfied and so they spend their entire lives chasing after something they will never really be capable of achieving. Epictetus knew that to be truly wealthy one must first be grateful for the wealth he owns and be satisfied with it.

Have you ever heard the saying that in a poor's house there's a lot more to share that a rich house? When people have fewer possessions, they understand their real value and importance and so they do not hesitate to share them with other people who might be in need. Rich people are more greedy with their money and possessions and are obsessed with keeping them intact, as if having a museum of stuff you don't use is the real test of happiness.

People who are less ambitious are more fulfilled, because they aren't always looking out for something else to make them feel satisfied. Since we know how important it is for the Stoics to have tranquility in our thoughts, constantly yearning for stuff is the opposite of apathies.

Learn to control your urges and desires and train yourself to see the value of the things that surround you. If you can only afford to eat out once a month, you will choose what you eat much more wisely and that meal will be much more delicious than if you were constantly going to a restaurant every day.

The Stoic secret is to live with little and be happy with it. Then, even if you get more things, they will seem like pleasant extras and not the stuff that gives your life meaning.

"For many men, the acquisition of wealth does not end their troubles, it only changes them" Seneca

Because Seneca lived his days in the heart of the Roman Empire and in the halls of power, surrounded by incredibly wealthy people, he knew that wealth could bring a lot more trouble. When you are poor, you worry about fulfilling your basic needs and worry about your health, strength and energy to sustain a job. You worry about getting your kids in school, finding a roof to put over their heads, buying stuff that makes life a little more comfortable.

When you become rich, you don't have the same kind of thoughts, but you are consumed by other types of worries. You need to learn to manage your money and position, to remain powerful and wealthy, to earn more gold to sustain a lavish lifestyle. You might alienate people you love and waste your days working to buy stuff you don't even need. Or you might be the object of envy and lose your ability to connect with people that are interested in you and not in your money.

Some people think that winning the lottery is the ticket for success and happiness. That the second they see those dollars in their bank account, all their worries will disappear. A true Stoic knows how mistaken these beliefs are. If you can't be happy with little, you'll be even more miserable when you have too much. Particularly because being wealthy can cause you to become less focused and disciplined, it can hinder your resistance and resilience and turn you into a soft and helpless creature.

"The only wealth you will keep forever is the wealth you have given away" Marcus Aurelius

When you are wealthy, it might be tempting to keep all the money to yourself so you can lavishly enjoy it and spend it in pleasurable things. But many millionaires, even today, realizethat wealth can be put to much better use if it becomes a legacy and if it provides less fortunate people with opportunities they never dreamed of.

When you give a large amount of money to charity or when you pay someone through higher education, the consequences of those actions will be much more far-fetching and long-lasting than if you had simply bought another flat screen TV.

Because the Stoics were people involved in the decision making of their own societies, Marcus Aurelius being the extreme example of that, they knew wealth was still important when it could be brought to accomplish a common good.

To keep wealth forever by giving away means using it to form a legacy that is not only yours, but of all people. If you use your wealth to invest in research, for example, even if it's just a tiny amount, you might have contributed to the cure of cancer of AIDS. Or if you give a few dollars to the building of that museum or gallery, you've assured future access to the arts for generations to come.

Knowing the power of wealth is knowing how much wonderful things can come of it when it's put to good use. In that way, the wealth you previously owned becomes eternal, something that is not only yours but of all people.

How to consider religion

We know Stoicism is a system of thought that still incorporates religion and that it has many religions parallels. So it's understanding that many Stoics wrote about their personal relationship with spirituality and the importance of religion, even though they distrusted the common folk religion of the Romans. Here are some thoughts on religion by our favorite philosophers:

"Religion is regarded by the common people as true, by the wise as false, and by rulers as useful." Seneca

This quote by Seneca seems custom-made for the XXI century. Today, many people around the world are distrustful of religion because they see it as a weapon of powerful people to control the weak and keep the common folk silent and obedient. The wisest religious people also share these intuitions, even though they might still believe in God, they know that the common image of God and the actions that are justified in His name are usually completely blasphemous.

Religion is still useful in the XXI century for rulers of many countries around the world to justify the biggest human rights atrocities and many uneducated people still consider religious dogmas to be the absolute truths. Philosophers don't have to be necessarily non-religious, but many maintain a healthy skepticism that allows them to appreciate events in the world through a clear and objective point of few, without the fear that God will punish them in some way.

"Live a good life. If there are gods and they are just, then they will not care how devout you have been, but will welcome you based on the virtues you have lived by. If there are gods, but unjust, then you should not want to worship them. If there are no gods, then you will be gone, but will have lived a noble life that will live on in the memories of your loved ones."
Marcus Aurelius

This quote by Marcus Aurelius embodies the healthiest attitude to be taken in regards toreligion, and one that many religious people would actually agree with.

It offers you three scenarios - one in which the Gods are just, one in which they are unjust and one in which they are nonexistent. And in all these scenarios the best course of action is to remain virtuous and true to yourself. Even if the Gods are wicked, that does not mean you should follow their example. If they aren't wicked, then they will appreciate your efforts to be virtuous even when you thought there was no reward and will provide you with the proper compensation. And if they don't exist, you still do - you still have to live in a world where you are faced with many difficult decisions and where you have to act in order to be alive.

In short, there is no bad outcome when you are virtuous. It is something you should always strive to do, and not because you think the Gods will be kind, but because it is something necessary for the proper functioning of the universe and of society. Having a good life is something completely dependent on yourself and not in some "friends" from above, so always be the best you can be, no excuses.

"He who exercises wisdom, exercises the knowledge which is about God." Epictetus

The term "God" in this quote should be understood in the context of Stoic metaphysics, as the principle of the universe and the logos that it its internal logic and order.

For the Stoics, when you are learning, you are learning about God in that sense. Since everything that surrounds you is a universe born out of the divine principle, everything is God.

This places an added burden upon your learning, since it means that you have to be extra careful when you are gathering knowledge to make sure it is the proper one. If you are learning about actions and beliefs that lead you against being virtuous, then you aren't learning about God. Every kind of truthful knowledge is God-like, so every time you learn something new you are getting closer and closer to God. The most religious man in the universe would be the Stoic Sage, who can live completely in accordance with the divine principles of apathies.

How to be better

Self-enhancement is one of the major goals of Stoic philosophy. You are always on a path to become a better human being, even though you can never really become the Stoic Sage. Here are our favorite quotes from our philosophers about that topics:

"We should every night call ourselves to an account: What infirmity have I mastered today? What passions opposed? What temptation resisted? What virtue acquired?" Seneca

You can only become better if you are constantly self-examining. Gathering your trophies and victories will lead to a narcissistic outlook on life unless you simultaneously collect your mistakes and errors, realizing where you can improve and where you can already feel slightly proud of yourself. Being proud is important insofar as it can motivate you to continue in your self-enhancement path.

If every night you go through the activities of your day, your feelings and emotions, and try to be completely honest with yourself, you'll soon understand there were many occasions where you could have acted better but many also where you could have acted worse. You'll learn where your self-control is more effective and draw on that experiences to improve yourself in other domains.

You can very well resist the passions of chocolate, but no so much those of married women? There's something to think about. You are virtuous when it comes to temperance, but not really when it comes to courage. Think deeply about your flaws and qualities on an everyday basis. Be vigilant regarding your own actions and thoughts. That's how you can slowly become better.

"It is impossible for a man to learn what he thinks he already knows." Epictetus

Many people will claim they want to improve themselves and then will start rambling about their endless convictions and knowledge that brought them to that desire and why they already are convinced of having found the ultimate truth. Or they will start taking new classes on issues that are of interest to them only to interrupt the professor at every turn, taking advantage to show what they think they know. When some presents them with new data on a given issue, they will answer your preconceived notions, trying to incorporate that data and distort it to fit with their ideas.

If you really want to be a better person, you have to start by accepting you don't know much. Maybe you are convinced that the best way to deal with a situation is to be angry or to be passive, but you don't have any real data to justify that belief. Or you are convinced that certain people are simply inferior because it was a belief handed to you after generations, but there's no scientific basis for that conviction.

People who have the love of wisdom - philosophers, if you will - are better listeners than talkers. They know there is too much in this world for it to be known in its totality, so they strive to gather new information from the people surrounding them. They don't have absolute truths kept in their pockets, but rather beliefs that will change according to new discoveries and experiences.

Sometimes, people will spend their entire lives feeling miserable without changing a thing about themselves or their convictions. They will convince themselves the problem lies in the outside world that is so resistant to comply with their beliefs. But to really become a Stoic you need to keep an open mind and an open heart that is not afraid of change, but yearns for it.

Every kind of learning can be of value. If you are to take advantage of those opportunities, you need to keep yourself open to new information and knowledge.

"Waste no more time arguing about what a good man should be. Be one." Marcus Aurelius

There are way too many people who spend most of their time criticizing other people's actions and cannot look at their own. In politics, it's common to discuss the best course of action and to denigrate your opponent based on their character, as if there was always this ideal of the perfect human being lying around for good example. But in truth, most of the critics prove by their own life experiences to be unable to respect that ideal.

If you keep re-thinking the actions of people around you, pointing out they should be better here or there, that the girl in the supermarket was rude even though you hadn't even cracked a smile, or that your professors can't be trusted even though it was the third time you asked to deliver your paper two days late, why should your opinion matter?

Being a good man is not just about having pretty words and nice ideas. It's about action, how you present yourself to others and how you can show yourself to be honest and reliable. If after reading this whole book you use it just to impress your friends but keep doing the same mistakes and having the same attitudes, you learned nothing about self-improvement.

Instead of wasting your time coming up with a tidy theory about the ethics of mankind, use those precious hours helping out your fellow men. Volunteer, educate yourself, give a friend a helping hand. Show that you care about ethics to the point of actually embodying it and become the ideal example for the people around you.

You'll notice that once you begin to change, other people will follow suit. It's much harder to be unethical when the general standard is high. But if you let the standard be low, no one will feel like they need to be held accountable for their action. Begin this revolution of taking responsibility for your own actions and your life will change for the better.

How to be disciplined

Much of the Stoic principles can only be observed if you are a disciplined person. Many of our philosophers had demanding lives and positions that forced them to take their duties extremely seriously, even if they preferred to spend their days contemplating the marvelous work of nature. Next time you're thinking about procrastinating, here are some wise words to listen to:

"Practice yourself, for heaven's sake in little things, and then proceed to greater." Epictetus

You want to win the marathon, but don't have enough discipline to run every day? Or you want to lose 100lbs, but aren't capable of resisting the most basic craving for sugar?

Epictetus knew most people will start their endeavors with grandioso illusions of big victories and will soon give up once they realize how impossible their dreams are. That's why he advises you to start small, with simple daily habits that will foster the skill of discipline. Like all other things, it's a learned skill - you need to begin somewhere, and you shouldn't bite more than you can chew.

Successful people start learning how to be disciplined early in life. They set up a routine and follow through, initially a study or exercise routine that develops into something more as their careers advance and they take up more responsibility. The Stoics knew the instinct of most people is to give up on discipline the second they have to start making sacrifices, even if you can hold on for the first days or weeks.

Don't aim to become chaste, healthy, bulk, knowledgeable on books and math all at once.

Decide the very particular skills you want to improve, set up a plan and follow through with it. Only afterwards can you begin to think about higher goals and try to achieve them.

For heaven's sake, don't try to be a hero in your first try. Trust Epictetus, a former slave who probably had to suffer a lot to find the required discipline to serve his master and master philosophy all at once.

"Do your duty
- and never mind whether you are shivering or warm, sleeping on your feet or in your bed, hearing yourself slandered or praised, dying, or doing something else.
Yes, even dying is an act of life and should be done, like everything else, "to the best of your abilities." Marcus Aurelius

No excuses, says Marcus Aurelius. Everybody has a bunch of duties in life they must respect. These can be related to parenting, family, job, school, community...the type does not matter, every kind of duty has to be done to the full extentof your abilities. Are you feeling sick, tired, sad? That's your problem - for the people depending on you, reality will not be kinder in case you want to take a break.

Many of our duties fell into the Stoic system as simply natural things that were a part of the order of the universe. Respecting the laws of your community meant being a proper creature in the cosmopolitan reality created by the divine. Being respectful to your parents while being a child and caring for them in old age was the natural cycle of life.

In today's world, many people try to evade their responsibilities by claiming it wasn't their job to do this in a certain way, that they are only paid to work 8 hours and not 8h15. Perhaps if everyone tried their best to do their share in the most perfect way possible we wouldn't be faced with so many troubles derived of negligence and lack of care.

We find this advice to be of particular interest to anyone working in the public sector and to anyone raising a child. There's simply too much at risk for you to miss your duties.

"Set aside a certain number of days, during which you shall be content with the scantiest and cheapest fare, with course and rough dress, saying to yourself the while: "Is this the condition that I feared?" Seneca

This is a funny advice from Seneca. Building resistance against the roughest environments is a part of discipline, a fact military schools can attest wholeheartedly. If you follow Seneca's words, you should live a few days every month in complete survival-mode. Go into the wild and learn to fend for yourself, to live in the cold without a proper winter jacket, to swim in natural streams that don't have a heating button. After doing that a few times, you'll be in the proper state of mind to wonder if that was indeed your worst fear, if everything falls through if living like that would really be the worst thing in the world.

Simple steps like that will make you resilient and have the necessary discipline to face the world. When you know and have felt and lived the worst case scenario, you are much better prepared to live in comfort and make the best of it.

Even though it might sound strange, many parents and educators know they value of this lesson and that's why they sometimes encourage children to go on volunteering missions abroad, to understand the lives of people who are less fortunate and learning how to live with little in terms of material possessions. It's a character-building lesson that can completely change your life.

How to be happy

Being happy is the end of Stoic ethics, so it's only natural our favorite philosophers had plenty to say on the subject. It always comes back to taking responsibility for your own happiness or misery and having the will to change your outlook on life.

"Man is not worried by real problems so much as by his imagined anxieties about real problems" Epictetus

You know by now how much of Stoic philosophy urges you to ignore your existential fear when you cannot control their outcome. For most people, especially those with anxiety disorders, the problems who make up yourself regarding your career, your personal life or your wealth lead you to become much more unhappier than if you just accepted that some things simply cannot be changed, and others are not yours to control.

Many people will become obsessed with scenarios they picture in their head. What if she doesn't love me? What if I am going to end up alone? What if my headache is actually a symptom of a much more worrying disease? And minutes, days, months go by in which you do not do any action to solve a potential problem, but simply worry about its hypothetical existence. It's a self-perpetuating self-sabotage technique, that does not make anything better.

Be a Stoic and stop worrying yourself with stuff that hasn't even happened yet.

"The happiness of your life depends upon the quality of your thoughts." Marcus Aurelius

Here is an insightful quote by Marcus Aurelius that sums up most of stoic philosophy when it comes to happiness. It's not enough to have cheerful thoughts, if they are based on nothing but falsehoods. What you must do to guarantee a happy life is focusing on improving your thoughts and fill them with knowledge. Knowledge of how to think and act - strive to be logical, objective, yet still empathetic towards your fellow men. Don't feed your most basic instincts of fearfulness, rage or sadness. Realize that the only person responsible for controlling your own happiness if yourself, because you are the person who is control of your thoughts. A new perspective on a given situation can alter completely your feelings regarding that situation, improving your overall well-being. Don't become obsessed with self-defeating and loath-filled thoughts, but instead fill your mind with objective feelings of gratefulness for everything you have accomplished so far.

"Where fear is, happiness is not." Seneca

If you are afraid, you are paralyzed. If you let yourself be dominated by the distress and pain of fear, there is no way you can cultivate either the virtues or the feelings necessary to become a well-round and fulfilled human being. As we've mentioned before, fear is negative feeling breeding misery. That does not being you must eliminate fear altogether and become totally fearless - as we've said, you still have to exercise a degree of caution in order to be a proper stoic.

Here's an example: you're stuck in a dead end job and you want to get rid of it as soon as possible. In one extreme, you will never have the guts to act because you are paralyzed by the fear of facing your boss and a life without a steady income. In the other extreme, you leave your job with a bang and seriously damage your chances of finding a new one, putting yourself and your loved ones at risk. A Stoic would understand that he cannot be controlled neither in control of reality, therefore, you must try to do the sensible thing. Prepare yourself in advance for the change of job and have a honest conversation with your boss, even if you hate the guy. Being honest, forthcoming and determined will lead you to make peace with yourself, while covering your bases will guarantee at least some degree of comfort while looking for a new job.

As long as you let fear dominate you, you will never be happy, but will be forever living in the shadows of your own nightmares. Sometimes, you simply have to man up and face the things that make you scared in order to break free.

Bonus chapter: The Stoics on love

This bonus chapter was added as a little of a provocation. Since we've covered so much of Stoic philosophy that focus on controlling emotions, what do our enlightened philosophers have to say when it comes to love? Although Marcus Aurelius had lovers and Seneca and Epictetus are thought to have been married at one point or another, each of them considered other parts of life to be of more importance. But that does not mean they weren't taken with love themselves or did not write about it.

After all, it's one of the sweetest, bitterest and most important parts of life for any human being.

The Stoics exercise caution when it comes to love. They know that a man in love- or in lust- is capable of mad things and that it can indeed enslave your mind. If you are looking for the apatheia of the Stoic Sage, you can't be constantly tormented with butterflies in your stomach. However, since we exist in a cosmopolitan community, a brotherhood of men, we must have some love drawing us closer to really feel like part of the community.

In short, we can say the Stoics valued love - the profound emotional connection that arises between human beings and provides your life with meaning - and were highly distrustful of passion.

The ideal form of love for the Stoics in one in which the tranquility of your mind remains undisturbed. Think about those increasingly few successful long marriages, in which both husband and wife are living together but apart, in which each of them is given enough space to focus on their own endeavors and turn to each other for comfort and pleasure as a bonus, a special thing that should not be taken for granted but makes life so much better.

Loving as a Stoic means recognizing that love and passion might be fleeting, that everything is transient and that your love will probably not remain eternal, but knowing you should still let yourself be taken care of by your special person and enjoy every single moment spent in their presence.

In the end, it might be the most romantic form of love. One that is still built on logical principles, but that is beautiful, like a picture caught in time. Remembering the fragility of things in the universe is knowing that love is a fleeting miracle that graces our lives and for which we should be grateful, without losing our minds. Only then can we truly appreciate the person we love and the feelings we feel towards them.

Chapter 8: Conclusion:

After reading this book, you've probably reached the conclusion that being a Stoic is hard work. That's true - many of the ideas we've shared with you are counter-intuitive in our society and you might struggle achieving all the goals we've advocated for in this book. But Stoicism is a centuries old philosophy that has never ceased to be influential, being re-invented and re-incorporated into reality by different generations of people throughout history.

We hope that this book has taught you the importance of conforming to your own reality and the importance of understanding how your emotions work. Some of them, as we've seen, are very positive, while others can be very damaging and indeed ruin your path to self-improvement.

We also hope you have understood the importance of freedom of will and how your ultimate happiness is always depending on you and you alone. The friends you choose, your careers, your relationships, the way you love someone and how you respond to adversity is always depending on the control you exercise over your own emotions and it is never the fault of the outside world. Even when dealing with people that can exasperate you, it is always your choice whether or not you will let yourself be disturbed or upset by them. Learn to manage your feels of anger and sadness and accept the truth that most things in this world are transient and fleeting, the ones that cause you to hurt and the ones that bring you joy.

There are many simple ideas you can use to implement stoicism in your daily life. We presented some of them to you, but as you continue your study of stoicism and read the major works by our favorite philosophers, you will come up with new strategies and habits of your own, turning stoicism into a very personal lifestyle that can bring your life meaning and teach you how to be resilient in the face of adversity.

You've also learned the opinions of our favorite philosophers regarding some of the common worries of human beings, such as wealth or religion. Think deeply about those topics and why they matter to you, how you can find a new and healthier understanding of them and always examine yourself and be vigilant of your actions, to make sure you do not deviate from the virtuous path.

Speaking about virtues, they are probably the most precious piece of knowledge in this book. You can throw the rest away if you think stoicism is too demanding for you, but cultivating the virtues is not such a hard thing and can indeed make your life and the life of those around you much better. It's the duty of every single one of us to do our best in life, do perform our duties with care and diligence, to meditate upon our thoughts and actions and how to improve them, and to better the general conditions of our society and of our fellow-men.

Now that you know Stoicism is not the heartless boogeyman some people think it is, spread the knowledge you acquired today with your friends. Hopefully, they will be the ideal Stoic friends, the kind that uplift you and make you want to be a better person. If not, then this is a good opportunity to meet new people who fit your needs and who can actually help you navigate this difficult challenge we call life.

We wish you the best in your future endeavors and we are grateful for taking the time to read this book. Hopefully, it was as fun to read as it was to write.

BIBLIOGRAPHY

Books by our philosophers:

Marcus Aurelius, *The Meditations*, translated by George Long, The Peter Pauper Press, 1957.

Seneca, *Letters From a Stoic*, translated by Robin Campbell, Penguin Books, 2004.

Seneca, *The Stoic Philosophy of Seneca: Essays and Letters,* W.W Norton & Co, 1968.

Epictetus, *The Discourses*, Everyman's Library, 1995.

Epictetus, *Enchiridon*, translated by George Long, P.E Matheson, 1916.

Books about Stoicism:

The Cambridge Companion to the Stoics, ed. Brian Inwood, Cambridge University Press, 2003.

Becker, L.C, A New Stoicism, Princeton University Press, 1998.